Artistic Adventures
STORIES

Kelly Burkholder

The Rourke Press, Inc.
Vero Beach, Florida 32964

PHOTO CREDITS:
© East Coast Studios: cover, pages 4, 6, 13, 15, 16, 17; © Eyewire: page 7;
© PhotoDisc: pages 18, 21, 22

PRODUCED & DESIGNED by East Coast Studios
eastcoaststudios.com

EDITORIAL SERVICES:
Pamela Schroeder

Library of Congress Cataloging-in-Publication Data

Burkholder, Kelly, 1970-
   Stories / Kelly Burkholder.
     p. cm. — (Artistic adventures)
   Includes bibliographical references and index.
   Summary: Discusses different kinds of writing, how to get ideas, practice writing, and editing and revising.
   ISBN 1-57103-356-4
   1. Authorship—Juvenile literature. [1. Authorship.] I. Title.

PN147 .B86 2000
808'.02—dc21

                                  00–025373

Printed in the USA

Contents

Fiction and Nonfiction

Everyone loves good stories. They are fun to hear, read, and write. There are many kinds of stories. A story can be true or made-up. A made-up story is called fiction. A true story is called nonfiction. Think of nonfiction as non false. That will help you remember what nonfiction means.

Stories help teach us about our environment.

Types of Stories

A descriptive (de SKRIPT iv) story tells you about something. Imagine biting into your favorite candy bar. How would you **describe** (dih SKRYB) the taste? You might say it was delicious, milk chocolate, gooey, or full of caramel and nuts. Someone reading your story can imagine the taste because of how you described it.

Our five senses—sight, hearing, touch, smell, and taste help us describe things.

This girl persuades her friend to trust her.

Another type of story is persuasive (per SWAY siv). In a persuasive story you try to make someone believe what you say. You have probably used persuasive stories many times. Think about how you try to make your parents let you do something. That is how persuasive stories work.

Expository (eks POS i tor ee) stories help you explain how to do something. Expository stories are like recipes. You use **transition** (tran ZISH en) words in expository stories. *First, second, next,* and *last* are transition words. Think of how you might tell someone how to make a peanut butter and jelly sandwich.

"To make a good peanut butter and jelly sandwich you must first start with two pieces of bread. Next, spread the peanut butter on one slice of bread. After that, spread the jelly on the other slice of bread. Put the two slices of bread together to make the sandwich. Last, cut the sandwich in half and enjoy."

Expository stories are like recipes. They give you step-by-step instructions.

Beginning

Once upon a time a lion was trying to get some sleep. A pesty, little mouse began running up and down the lion's mane. This soon awakened the lion. The lion, still tired and now grumpy, grabbed the mouse and thought about hurting him. The mouse cried for forgiveness and told the lion that if he lets him go free someday he may be able to help the lion. How could a little mouse help him, the king of the jungle? He was so tickled at the idea of the mouse being able to help him, that he lifted up his paw and let him go.

Middle

Some time later the lion was caught in a trap, and the hunters were taking him to the King as a gift. While the hunters looked for the cart to carry the lion, they tied him up to a tree to prevent him from escaping. Just then the mouse happened to be walking by, and seeing the lion tied to the tree, remembered how the lion showed him mercy by setting him free. The mouse went up to the lion and began to chew away at the rope.

End

After gnawing on the rope for several minutes the lion was free. He thanked his new friend, the mouse. They promised to always remain friends.

Narrative (NAR a tiv) stories are also very popular. Many of the books you read are narrative. A narrative story has a beginning. That is where you meet the characters. It also has a middle. The middle of a story tells what happens to the characters. Finally, a narrative story must have an ending.

An example of a narrative story is *Snow White and the Seven Dwarfs*. In the beginning you meet Snow White and the Wicked Witch. In the middle you learn that the Wicked Witch wants Snow White dead. She casts a spell on Snow White with a poison apple. Last, you read the ending. The Prince kisses Snow White. She wakes up from the magic spell and they live happily ever after.

This is another example of a narrative story.

Finding an Idea

Finding an idea can be the hardest part of writing a story. Most writers say you should write about what you know. If you write about what you know, or what you love, you can't go wrong. You can write nonfiction about your own life, or something you like to do. Or you can make something up and write fiction.

There are good story ideas all around us.

Ready, Set, Write

What do you do when you get an idea? Try to keep a notebook with you so you can write down all your great ideas. What do you like to write about? What kind of writing is the most fun for you? Do you like scary stories, funny stories, or stories about the future? If it's fun for you to write, it will be fun for others to read. **Experiment** (ek SPEER eh ment) with writing different kinds of stories.

Find out what kind of stories you like to read.

How can you get better? Write something every day. It doesn't have to be great. It just has to be something. If you don't have a story idea that you like, write about your day. What made you laugh? How did you feel? What happened at school? Make writing a **habit** (HAB it) that you do every day.

The beach is a good place to write in your journal.

Reading a lot helps you become a good writer.

Read a lot. The more you read, the more you will learn about good writing. Think about what you like and don't like about the books you read. Write to your favorite authors and ask them for writing tips.

Edit and Revise

Now that you are a writer, you need to learn to **edit** (ED it) and **revise** (ree VYZ). When you edit your story, you check spelling and **grammar** (GRAM er). You also make sure you have your facts right.

You also should revise your story. Revising a story does not mean correcting spelling. Revising means taking another look at your story. If you don't like everything about your story, you can change it. Don't worry. Most writers say they edit and revise one story many times.

Editing and revising is something all writers do.

Writer's Group

Do you have any friends who like to write? You can make a writer's group where you help each other. You can read each other's stories. Then share your **opinions** (uh PIN yunz) about them. Sometimes it helps to hear what others think about what you write. It is nice to hear what your friends have to say.

A writer's group is a great place to share ideas and stories.

Glossary

describe (dih SKRYB) — to give more information about something; using words to give someone a better picture of something in their mind

edit (ED it) — to check your writing to make sure it is correct

experiment (ek SPEER eh ment) — to try new and different things

grammar (GRAM er) — rules for making sentences

habit (HAB it) — something that you do a lot

opinion (uh PIN yun) — how you feel or what you think about something

revise (ree VYZ) — to change your story until you are happy with what you have written

transition (tran ZISH en) — a way to change from one thing to the next

A writer works on a computer to write her story.

Index

Further Reading

Find out more about stories with these helpful information sites:

www.KidPub.com
www.YoungAuthor'sWorkshop.com
www.YoungWriter'sClubhouse.com